THE TRUTH ABOUT WRITING

ABRAMS NOTERIE, NEW YORK

THIS STORY
IN MY HEAD
IS TOO HOT
TO TOUCH.

I GRABBED IT
ANYWAY.

ADELE GRIFFIN

ON THE CRAFTING OF WORDS

We writers are crafty people: We practice an ancient and honored craft by crafting sentences that can inform, entertain, and arouse readers. And, at times, we also write squibs intended to cover our own hindquarters.

Our trade is the only one of the classic arts which, by the very practice of our craft, we can explain, elaborate, correct, even defend and stump for our efforts. A sculptor can't chisel why he chose to use Carrara rather than Parian marble, a composer can't in musical notes expound on why her symphony lacks a scherzo, nor can a painter limn a defense of personal theories about line, color, and form. We're historically—and always at our core—storytellers; yet, with a single word we can cease spinning yarns for philosophizing on whatever the devil flits through our brains (such as why we're writing what we're writing in the first place); we can interrupt our tale by theorizing on whatever might clarify, intensify, or indemnify it.

In my books, I've long wished to preempt an expected critical comment by, say, thwarting a complaint about the vocabulary of my writing at times possibly being needlessly esoteric. I've wanted to say, "Come on, dear readers! Relax and have some fun! Maybe even pick up a damn dictionary and look up a word!" Vocabulary building is gratifying. I haven't actually written those words until just this moment, but I'm happy now to have had the chance at last to set them loose. So you see, capable reader, in this paragraph I'm doing the very thing I'm talking about: demonstrating—if not proving—my contention: Writers are crafty folk.

This collection of literary delights from more than 270 writers—that term here meaning anyone who has written poignantly on some aspect of writing—does, of course, address other components of our naturally apothegmatic craft. Within these pages you'll find maxims, aphorisms, adages, gnomes, axioms, scholia, bromides, principles, and even a number of self-evident truths. The best are pungent, eloquent, profound, indelible, amusing, heartfelt, and perhaps most important, truthful. I didn't happen upon any I consider utter bunkum. (Well, there was one.)

If you're beginning the craft of verbal composition, you'll likely come upon several notions able to help you along toward becoming the writer you dream of being. My own experience of learning to write was largely directed by well-intentioned instructors who had no practical experience beyond office memos, grocery lists, or letters to a kid at camp, as well as by editors whose familiarity with the classics of our language was scarcely beyond a high school survey course in English literature. During those apprentice years I encountered wordsmiths who knew the proven classics, scriveners who understood how it is that words can move from the mundane to the immortal. Some of such counsel is within these pages.

This collection can be a pocket companion dedicated to crafting ideas into well-turned phrasings, and it's also an alert to inherent pitfalls, challenges, agonies, and (occasionally) the triumphs of language wedded to emotion, truth, and yes, indeed, beauty.

—*William Least Heat-Moon*

ON BEING A WRITER

Who am I? What right have I to speak?
Who will listen to me if I do?
You're a human being, with a unique
story to tell, and you have every right.
If you speak with passion,
many of us will listen.
We need stories to live, all of us.
We live by story.
Yours enlarges the circle.

RICHARD RHODES

You write for the people in
high school who ignored you.
We all do it.

—CAROLYN KIZER

Who wants to become a
writer? And why? Because
it's the answer to everything.
It's the streaming reason for
living. To note, to pin down,
to build up, to create, to be
astonished at nothing, to
cherish the oddities, to let
nothing go down the drain, to
make something, to make a
great flower out of life, even if
it's a cactus.

—ENID BAGNOLD

We write to taste life twice, in
the moment and in retrospect.

—ANAÏS NIN

(contributed by Marisa Siegel, *The Rumpus*)

Writers will happen in the best
of families.

—RITA MAE BROWN

Most of the basic material a
writer works with is acquired
before the age of fifteen.

—WILLA CATHER

IF I HAD ALWAYS SLEPT
PROPERLY, I'D NEVER HAVE
WRITTEN A LINE.

LOUIS-FERDINAND CÉLINE

Writing is not like dancing or modeling; it's not something where—if you missed it by age nineteen—you're finished. It's never too late. Your writing will only get better as you get older and wiser. If you write something beautiful and important, and the right person somehow discovers it, they will clear room for you on the bookshelves of the world—at any age.

ELIZABETH GILBERT

Writers have this narcissistic
obsession about how we got
to be who we are.

—SANDRA CISNEROS

I write because I cannot
not write.

—CHARLOTTE BRONTË

I love being a writer. What I
can't stand is the paperwork.

—PETER DE VRIES

Words, so innocent
and powerless as they are,
as standing in a dictionary,
how potent for good and evil
they become in the hands
of one who knows how to
combine them.

—NATHANIEL HAWTHORNE

I tend to believe all writers are cartographers and we are mapping human experiences.

—ROXANE GAY

If you were a member of Jesse James' band and people asked you what you were, you wouldn't say, "Well, I'm a desperado." You'd say something like "I work in banks" or "I've done some railroad work." It took me a long time just to say, "I'm a writer." It's really embarrassing.

—ROY BLOUNT, JR.

As far as I'm concerned, the entire reason for becoming a writer is not having to get up in the morning.

—NEIL GAIMAN

The writer is a mysterious figure, wandering lonely as a cloud, fired by inspiration, or perhaps a cocktail or two.

—SARA SHERIDAN

I WRITE...

. . . **BECAUSE** I am curious. I am curious about me.

—PAT MORA

. . . **TO** become someone else—that better, smarter self that lives inside my dumbstruck twin.

—DORIANNE LAUX

. . . **BECAUSE** I'm afraid to say some things out loud.

—GORDAN ATKINSON

. . . **TO** save someone's life, probably my own.

—CLARICE LISPECTOR

You're not going into the I'm-a-born-newspaperman-with-ink-in-my-veins-instead-of-blood speech, are you?

—WHIT MASTERSON

Getting even is one reason for writing.

—WILLIAM H. GASS

Find out the reason that commands you to write; see whether it has spread its roots into the very depth of your heart; confess to yourself you would have to die if you were forbidden to write.

—RAINER MARIA RILKE

Everywhere I go, I find a poet has been there before me.

—SIGMUND FREUD

Being a writer is like having
homework every night for the
rest of your life.

—LAWRENCE KASDAN

Resign yourself to the lifelong
sadness that comes from
never being satisfied.

—ZADIE SMITH

IF IT DOESN'T FEEL AT SOME POINT LIKE PEELING OFF YOUR OWN SKIN, YOU'RE PROBABLY NOT BEING HONEST ENOUGH.

MELISSA FEBOS

IF YOU AREN'T GONNA SAY EXACTLY HOW AND WHAT YOU FEEL, YOU MIGHT AS WELL NOT SAY ANYTHING AT ALL.

JOHNNY CASH

A poet is a man who manages, in a lifetime of standing out in thunderstorms, to be struck by lightning five or six times.

—RANDALL JARRELL

Poetry creates the myth, the prose writer draws its portrait.

—JEAN-PAUL SARTRE

I remember that it bothered my father very much that I wanted to write. With the best of intentions, he thought that writing would bring destruction to the family and myself and, especially, that it would lead me to a life of complete uselessness.

—PABLO NERUDA

I think I did pretty well,
considering I started out
with nothing but a bunch
of blank paper.

—STEVE MARTIN

When I would write fiction,
I would make up things,
and people wondered. No
matter what I do, it makes
people wonder. I think that's
just my job.

—A.M. HOMES

A bird doesn't sing because it has an answer, it sings because it has a song.

—MAYA ANGELOU

As a writer you are free. You are about the freest person that ever was. Your freedom is what you have bought with your solitude.

—URSULA K. LE GUIN

Why does one begin to write? Because she feels misunderstood, I guess. Because it never comes out clearly enough when she tries to speak. Because she wants to rephrase the world, to take it in and give it back again differently, so that everything is used and nothing is lost.

—NICOLE KRAUSS

SOME AMERICAN WRITERS
WHO HAVE KNOWN
EACH OTHER FOR YEARS
HAVE NEVER MET IN THE
DAYTIME OR WHEN BOTH
WERE SOBER.

JAMES THURBER

When I sit down to write a book, I do not say to myself, "I am going to produce a work of art." I write it because there is some lie that I want to expose, some fact to which I want to draw attention, and my initial concern is to get a hearing.

GEORGE ORWELL

To live a creative life we must
first lose the fear of being
wrong.

— JOSEPH CHILTON PEARCE

I think new writers are too
worried that it has all been said
before. Sure it has, but not
by you.

— ASHA DORNFEST

There are no dull subjects.
There are only dull writers.

— H. L. MENCKEN

ONE OF THE...

. . . **THINGS** that draws writers to writing is that they can get things right that they got wrong in real life . . .

—TOBIAS WOLFF

. . . **DISADVANTAGES** of wine is that it makes a man mistake words for thoughts.

—SAMUEL JOHNSON

. . . **REALLY** bad things you can do to your writing is to dress up the vocabulary, looking for long words because you're maybe a little bit ashamed of your short ones.

—STEPHEN KING

But that's what writers do.
We sit in our darknesses and
sometimes out emerges light.

—IRA SUKRUNGRUANG

A major writer combines
these three—storyteller,
teacher, enchanter—but it
is the enchanter in him that
predominates and makes him
a major writer.

—VLADIMIR NABOKOV

If you're a singer, you lose your
voice. A baseball player loses
his arm. A writer gets more
knowledge, and if he's good,
the older he gets, the better
he writes.

—MICKEY SPILLANE

Everybody walks past a thousand story ideas every day. The good writers are the ones who see five or six of them. Most people don't see any.

—ORSON SCOTT CARD

Having imagination, it takes you an hour to write a paragraph that, if you were unimaginative, would take you only a minute.

—FRANKLIN P. ADAMS

Stories have given me a place in which to lose myself. They have allowed me to remember. They have allowed me to forget. They have allowed me to imagine different endings and better possible worlds.

—ROXANE GAY

THERE IS NO GREATER AGONY THAN BEARING AN UNTOLD STORY INSIDE OF YOU.

MAYA ANGELOU

(contributed by Donna Talarico, *Hippocampus*)

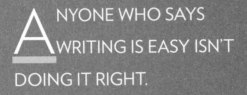

ANYONE WHO SAYS
WRITING IS EASY ISN'T
DOING IT RIGHT.

AMY JOY

YOU...

... **DON'T** write because you want to say something,
you write because you've got something to say.

—F. SCOTT FITZGERALD

(contributed by Lee Gutkind, *Creative Nonfiction*)

... **CAN'T** wait for inspiration.
You have to go after it with a club.

—JACK LONDON

... **LEARN** by writing short stories. Keep writing
short stories. The money's in novels, but writing
short stories keeps your writing lean and pointed.

—LARRY NIVEN

. . . **WRITE** to communicate to the hearts and minds of others what's burning inside you. And we edit to let the fire show through the smoke.

—ARTHUR PLOTNIK
(contributed by Dinty Moore, *Brevity*)

. . . **DON'T** give people what they want. You give them what they don't yet know they want.

—MO WILLEMS

. . . **WILL** feel insecure and jealous. How much power you give those feelings is entirely up to you.

—CHERYL STRAYED
(contributed by Dinty Moore, *Brevity*)

A WRITER'S LIFE IS NOT DESIGNED TO REASSURE YOUR MOTHER.

RITA MAE BROWN

If you have any young friends who aspire to become writers, the second greatest favor you can do them is to present them with copies of *The Elements of Style*. The first greatest, of course, is to shoot them now, while they're happy.

DOROTHY PARKER

If you're a poet, you do
something beautiful. I mean,
you're supposed to leave
something beautiful after
you get off the page and
everything.

—J.D. SALINGER
(contributed by Marisa Siegel, *The Rumpus*)

Whatever art offered the
men and women of previous
eras, what it offers our own,
it seems to me, is space—a
certain breathing room for the
spirit.

—JOHN UPDIKE
(contributed by Elliot Figman, *Poets&Writers*)

Most writers regard the
truth as their most valuable
possession, and therefore are
most economical in its use.

—MARK TWAIN

The writer experiences
everything twice. Once in
reality and once in the mirror
which waits always before
or behind.

—CATHERINE DRINKER
BOWEN

Be obscure clearly.

—E.B. WHITE

It's never too late to be what
you might have been.

   —GEORGE ELIOT

The everyday reader loves
reading true stories by real
people . . . they give us hope.

   —DONNA TALARICO,
    Hippocampus

Women have always been
poor, not for two hundred
years merely, but from
the beginning of time. . . .
Women, then, have not had a
dog's chance of writing poetry.
That is why I have laid so
much stress on money and a
room of one's own.

   —VIRGINIA WOOLF

I think writing really helps you heal yourself. I think if you write long enough you will be a healthy person. That is if you write what you need to write. As opposed to what will make money, or what will make fame.

ALICE WALKER

3 GUYS ARE SITTING AT A BAR

The first says, "Yeah, I make $275,000 a year after taxes."

Second says, "What do you do for a living?"

First replies, "I'm a stockbroker. How much do you make?"

Second answers, "I should clear $160,000. I'm an architect."

The two of them turn to third guy, who is quietly staring into his beer, and ask him how much he makes per year.

Third guys says, "I guess about $3,000."

First says, "Oh yeah? What kind of stories do you write?"

I heard some writer say that his "father was a truck driver, and you know what, never in his life did that man get truck driver's block."

—BARNABY CONRAD

If art doesn't make us better, then what on earth is it for?

—ALICE WALKER
(contributed by Elliot Figman, *Poets&Writers*)

Life is the most productive part of a writer's life.

—JAMES NORMAN HALL

All my best thoughts were stolen by the ancients.

—attributed to
RALPH WALDO EMERSON

WRITING IS
THE ONLY
PROFESSION
WHERE NO ONE
CONSIDERS YOU
RIDICULOUS
IF YOU EARN
NO MONEY.

JULES RENARD

A WRITER IS..

... A WORLD trapped in a person.

—VICTOR HUGO

... SOMEBODY for whom writing is more difficult than it is for other people.

—THOMAS MANN

... A PERSON who cares what words mean, what they say, how they say it.

—URSULA K. LE GUIN
(contributed by Sarah Hill, *Bookstr*)

... A WRITER because, even when there is no hope, even when nothing you do shows any sign of promise, you keep writing anyway.

—JUNOT DÍAZ
(contributed by Dinty Moore, *Brevity*)

All writers are a little crazy but if they are any good they have a kind of terrible honesty.

RAYMOND CHANDLER

Writers seem to me to be people who need to retire from social life and do a lot of thinking about what's happened, almost to calm themselves.

—HELEN GARNER

A good writer is always a people watcher.

—JUDY BLUME

Nothing quite has reality for me till I write it all down— revising and embellishing as I go. I'm always waiting for things to be over so I can get home and commit them to paper.

—ERICA JONG

IF WRITERS WERE GOOD BUSINESSMEN, THEY'D HAVE TOO MUCH SENSE TO BE WRITERS.

IRVIN S. COBB

IF THE DOCTOR TOLD ME
I HAD SIX MINUTES TO LIVE,
I'D TYPE FASTER.

ISAAC ASIMOV

As children, some of us liked magic and fantasy more than reality. So we became writers.

—DR. SUNWOLF

If one is lucky, a solitary fantasy can totally transform one million realities.

—MAYA ANGELOU
(contributed by Elliot Figman, *Poets&Writers*)

If a nation loses its storytellers, it loses its childhood.

—PETER HANDKE
(contributed by Donna Talarico, *Hippocampus*)

A writer, I think,
is someone who pays
attention to the world.

—SUSAN SONTAG

Remember,
rewriting is redemption.

—WILLIAM LEAST HEAT-MOON

I write in order to attain that
feeling of tension relieved and
function achieved which a cow
enjoys on giving milk.

—H. L. MENCKEN

Writing is something you do
alone. It's a profession for
introverts who wanna tell you
a story but don't wanna make
eye contact while telling it.

—JOHN GREEN

I strongly believe that writing
an act of courage. It's almost
an act of physical courage.

—TA-NEHISI COATES

The beautiful part of writing
is that you don't have to get it
right the first time, unlike, say,
a brain surgeon.

—ROBERT CORMIER

Writing is communication, not
self-expression; nobody in this
world wants to read your diary,
except your mother.

—RICHARD PECK

Writers spend three years rearranging twenty-six letters of the alphabet. It's enough to make you lose your mind day by day.

RICHARD PRICE

The real beauty of being
a writer is that you can work
in bed.

—NANCY DEVILLE

The writer should never be
ashamed of staring. There is
nothing that does not require
his attention.

—FLANNERY O'CONNOR

What no wife of a writer can
ever understand is that a writer
is working when he's staring
out of the window.

—BURTON RASCOE

Writers see the world differently. Every voice we hear, every face we see, every hand we touch could become story fabric.

—BUFFY ANDREWS

When you're writing, you're trying to find out something which you don't know.

—JAMES BALDWIN

Writers don't write from experience . . . writers write from empathy.

—NIKKI GIOVANNI

The greatest sin for a writer is to be boring.

—CARL HIAASEN

The Mailer ego, the Buckley wit. . . .

Bill Buckley sent a copy of his latest book to Norman Mailer. Disappointed to discover that Buckley had not personally inscribed the book, Mailer turned instead to the index to see if he was mentioned in the book. Next to Mailer's name in the index was the handwritten greeting, "Hi!"

I embrace the label of bad feminist because I am human. I am messy. I'm not trying to be an example. I am not trying to be perfect. I am not trying to say I have all the answers. I am not trying to say I'm right. I am just trying—trying to support what I believe in, trying to do some good in this world, trying to make some noise with my writing while also being myself.

ROXANE GAY

(contributed by Marisa Siegel, *The Rumpus*)

The useless days will add up to something.

The shitty waitressing jobs.

The hours writing in your journal.

The long meandering walks.

The hours reading poetry and story collections and novels. . . .

These things are your becoming.

CHERYL STRAYED

ON GETTING STARTED

So, okay. There you are in your room with the shade down and the door shut and the plug pulled out of the base of the telephone. You've blown up your TV and committed yourself to a thousand words a day, come hell or high water. Now comes the big question: What are you going to write about? And the equally big answer: Anything you damn well want.

STEPHEN KING

(contributed by Sarah Hill, *Bookstr*)

There's no such thing as writer's block. That was invented by people in California who couldn't write.

—TERRY PRATCHETT

My prescription for writer's block: Write badly. Bad writing is easier. And it must be popular, there's so much of it.

—P. J. O'ROURKE

Writer's block is a luxury most people with deadlines don't have.

—DIANE ACKERMAN

Sometimes my first written words are: "I don't know what to write."

—MERIDETH MEHLBERG

Delay is natural to a writer.
I walk around, straightening
pictures on the wall, rugs on
the floor—as though not until
everything in the world is lined
up and perfectly true could
anybody reasonably expect
me to set a word down on
paper.

—E.B. WHITE

I don't begin with a theme
or even a character. I begin
with a first sentence that is
independent of any conscious
preparation.

—JOSEPH HELLER

Creativity is allowing yourself
to make mistakes. Art is
knowing which ones to keep.

—SCOTT ADAMS

If you can tell stories, create
characters, devise incidents,
and have sincerity and passion,
it doesn't matter a damn how
you write.

—SOMERSET MAUGHAM

It is my ambition to say in ten
sentences what others say in a
whole book.

—FRIEDRICH NIETZSCHE

Friends visited Gustave Flaubert on a Friday, asking him to join their weekend trip. Flaubert declined, claiming he had work to do. When the friends returned on Sunday evening, Flaubert reported that work had gone very well. Yet the friends saw he was at exactly the same place he was when they left—in the middle of a sentence, marked by a comma. Flaubert noted that on Saturday he changed the comma to a semicolon, and on Sunday he changed it back, thus making wonderful progress.

I'm writing an unauthorized
autobiography.

—STEVEN WRIGHT

Do not wait for an idea. Start
writing something and the
ideas will come. You have to
turn the faucet on before the
water starts to flow.

—LOUIS L'AMOUR

Keep scribbling! Something
will happen.

—FRANK MCCOURT

A blank piece of paper is
God's way of telling us how
hard it is to be God.

—SIDNEY SHELDON

The blank page gives the right
to dream.

—GASTON BACHELARD

I have always had more dread
of a pen, a bottle of ink, and a
sheet of paper than of a sword
or pistol.

—ALEXANDRE DUMAS

To write feels better than all
the excuses.

—NATALIE GOLDBERG

I write to give myself strength.
I write to be the characters
that I am not. I write to explore
all the things I'm afraid of.

—JOSS WHEDON

How can you write
if you can't cry?

—RING LARDNER

I type in one place, but I write all over the house.

—TONI MORRISON

The best time for planning a book is while you're doing the dishes.

—AGATHA CHRISTIE

All my major works have been written in prison. . . . I would recommend prison not only to aspiring writers but to aspiring politicians, too.

—JAWAHARLAL NEHRU

Planning to write is not writing. Outlining a book is not writing. Researching is not writing. Talking to people about what you're doing, none of that is writing. Writing is writing.

—E. L. DOCTOROW

You only learn to be a better writer by actually writing.

—DORIS LESSING

Writer's block is only a failure of the ego.

—NORMAN MAILER

I believe, more than anything, that this grief of constantly having to face down our own inadequacies is what keeps people from being writers. Forgiveness, therefore, is key. I can't write the book I want to write, but I can and will write the book I am capable of writing. Again and again throughout the course of my life I will forgive myself.

ANN PATCHETT

Cats are dangerous
companions for writers
because cat watching is a
near-perfect method of
writing avoidance.

—DAN GREENBURG

Authors like cats because they
are such quiet, lovable, wise
creatures, and cats like authors
for the same reasons.

—ROBERTSON DAVIES

Do you realize that all great literature is all about what a bummer it is to be a human being?

—KURT VONNEGUT

I can't understand why a person will take a year to write a novel when he can easily buy one for a few dollars.

—FRED ALLEN

Take five ice cubes, place in clean glass, add vodka.

—PHIL MUSHNICK,
on overcoming writer's block

Booze, pot, too much sex, failure in one's private life, too much attrition, too much recognition, too little recognition. Nearly everything in the scheme of things works to dull a first-rate talent. But the worst probably is cowardice.

NORMAN MAILER

To produce a mighty book, you must choose a mighty theme.

HERMAN MELVILLE

What's so hard about that first sentence is that you're stuck with it. Everything else is going to flow out of that sentence. And by the time you've laid down the first two sentences, your options are all gone.

JOAN DIDION

I love writing. I love the swirl
and swing of words as they
tangle with human emotions.

—JAMES MICHENER

The secret of getting ahead is
getting started.

—MULTIPLE

The thing all writers do best is
find ways to avoid writing.

—ALAN DEAN FOSTER

Ideas are like rabbits. You get
a couple and learn how to
handle them, and pretty soon
you have a dozen.

—JOHN STEINBECK

If you wait for inspiration
to write, you're not a writer,
you're a waiter.

—DAN POYNTER

The first goal of writing is
to have one's words read
successfully.

—ROBERT BREAULT

I write entirely to find out what
I'm thinking, what I'm looking
at, what I see and what it
means. What I want and what
I fear.

—JOAN DIDION

The job of the first eight
pages is not to have the
reader want to throw the book
at the wall, during the first
eight pages.

—DAVID FOSTER WALLACE

First, find out what your hero
wants, then just follow him!

—RAY BRADBURY

All the information you need
can be given in dialogue.

—ELMORE LEONARD

Dialog is not just quotation.
It is grimaces, pauses,
adjustments of blouse buttons,
doodles on a napkin, and
crossings of legs.

—JEROME STERN

If you are using dialogue—say
it aloud as you write it. Only
then will it have the sound
of speech.

—JOHN STEINBECK

There is no artifice as good
and desirable as simplicity.

—ST. FRANCIS DE SALES

We write by the light of every
story we have ever read.

—RICHARD PECK

There are thousands of
thoughts lying within a man
that he does not know till he
takes up the pen and writes.

—WILLIAM MAKEPEACE
THACKERAY

I try to create
sympathy for
my characters,
then turn the
monsters loose.

STEPHEN KING

IT'S DOUBTFUL THAT ANYONE WITH AN INTERNET CONNECTION AT HIS WORKPLACE IS WRITING GOOD FICTION.

JONATHAN FRANZEN

WHEN I WAS A LITTLE BOY THEY CALLED ME A LIAR BUT NOW THAT I AM GROWN UP THEY CALL ME A WRITER.

ISAAC BASHEVIS SINGER

We who make stories know that we tell lies for a living. But they are good lies that say true things, and we owe it to our readers to build them as best we can. Because somewhere out there is someone who needs that story. Someone who will grow up with a different landscape, who without that story will be a different person. And who with that story may have hope, or wisdom, or kindness, or comfort.

And that is why we write.

NEIL GAIMAN

(contributed by Sarah Hill, *Bookstr*)

ON WRITING

As a writer, I need an enormous amount of time alone. Writing is 90 percent procrastination: reading magazines, eating cereal out of the box, watching infomercials. It's a matter of doing everything you can to avoid writing, until it is about four in the morning and you reach the point where you have to write. Having anybody watching that or attempting to share it with me would be grisly.

PAUL RUDNIK

I think . . . the most brilliant thing about being a writer is that if you don't like the way the world is, you can create your own.

—MAEGAN COOK

It's not a career for anyone who needs security. It's a career for gamblers. It's a career of ups and downs.

—GEORGE R.R. MARTIN

It ain't whatcha write, it's the way atcha write it.

—JACK KEROUAC
(contributed by Lee Gutkind,
Creative Nonfiction)

There is something delicious
about writing the first words of a
story. You never quite know
where they'll take you.

BEATRIX POTTER

There is no excuse. If you want to write, write. This is your life. You are responsible for it. You will not live forever. Don't wait. Make the time now.

—NATALIE GOLDBERG

Whatever our theme in writing, it is old and tried. Whatever our place, it has been visited by the stranger, it will never be new again. It is only the vision that can be new; but that is enough.

—EUDORA WELTY

And by the way, everything in life is writable about if you have the outgoing guts to do it, and the imagination to improvise. The worst enemy to creativity is self-doubt.

—SYLVIA PLATH
(contributed by Sarah Hill, *Bookstr*)

Write in a way that scares
you a little.

               —HOLLEY GERTH

It's hell writing and it's hell not
writing. The only tolerable
state is having just written.

               —ROBERT HASS

Writing a novel is a terrible
experience, during which
the hair often falls out and
the teeth decay. I'm always
irritated by people who imply
that writing fiction is an escape
from reality. It is a plunge into
reality and it's very shocking to
the system.

               —FLANNERY O'CONNOR

People will tell you that writing is too difficult, that it's impossible to get your work published, that you might as well hang yourself. Meanwhile, they'll keep writing and you'll have hanged yourself.

JOHN GARDNER

Concentrate on what you want to say to yourself and your friends. Follow your inner moonlight; don't hide the madness. You say what you want to say when you don't care who's listening.

ALLEN GINSBERG

THREE ¢ENTS A WORD

Early in his career, Erle Stanly Gardner was paid by the word to write for pulp magazines. The longer the story, the more he was paid. When Gardner's editor asked him why his heroes were such lousy shots, always killing the villains with the very last bullet in the gun, Gardner replied, "At three cents a word, every time I say bang in the story I get three cents. If you think I'm going to finish the gun battle while my hero has got fifteen cents' worth of unexploded ammunition in his gun, *you're nuts.*"

Some people do not seem to grasp that I still have to sit down in peace and write the books, apparently believing that they pop up like mushrooms without my connivance.

—J. K. ROWLING

I work every day on a very rigorous schedule. I do not procrastinate. Sometimes the work goes well, in which case I might end up with a paragraph or two of decent prose; other times the work goes badly, in which case I end up with a foul temper.

—TIM O'BRIEN

For I am a bear of very
little brain and long words
bother me.

—WINNIE THE POOH,
by A. A. Milne

Pithy sentences are like
sharp nails driving truth into
our memory.

—DIDEROT

I want to write books that
unlock the traffic jam in
everybody's head.

—JOHN UPDIKE

I never type in the morning. I don't get up in the morning. I drink at night. I try to stay in bed until twelve o'clock, that's noon. I eat something, and then I usually run right up to the race track. . . . I bet the horses, then I come back and Linda cooks something and we talk awhile, we eat, and we have a few drinks, and then I go upstairs with a couple of bottles and I type—starting around nine-thirty and going until one-thirty, to, two-thirty at night. And that's it.

CHARLES BUKOWSKI

Fiction is about stuff that's
screwed up.

—NANCY KRESS

Writers get ideas all day every
day. The FedEx guy delivers
a package from Sears and the
writer is thinking how it could
actually be a ticking time bomb.

—DAN ALATORRE

When I'm writing fiction, I'm
not thinking about "issues"
that I want to tackle. I have
a story idea and I write it. It's
just about storytelling.

—ROXANE GAY

I don't really write with an audience in mind. I write for myself and hope someone else likes to read it.

—JILLIAN MEDOFF

Writing is an extreme privilege but it's also a gift. It's a gift to yourself and it's a gift of giving a story to someone.

—AMY TAN

Writing, at its best and truest, can offer solace and salvation for both readers and writers.

—ROXANE GAY

Writers know words are their way towards truth and freedom, and so they use them with care, with thought, with fear, with delight.

—URSULA K. LE GUIN

Action is the thing. We are
what we do and do not do.

—RALPH ELLISON

. . . the truest writers are those
who see language not as a
linguistic process but as a
living element. . . ."

—DEREK WALCOTT
(contributed by Elliot Figman, *Poets&Writers*)

. . . write only what kicks you
and keeps you overtime awake
from sheer mad joy.

—JACK KEROUAC
(contributed by Marisa Siegel, *The Rumpus*)

Good fiction's job is to
comfort the disturbed and
disturb the comfortable.

—DAVID FOSTER WALLACE

The writer has to take the most used, most familiar objects—nouns, pronouns, verbs, adverbs—ball them together and make them bounce, turn them a certain way and make people get into a romantic mood; and another way, into a bellicose mood.

MAYA ANGELOU

A good style should show
no sign of effort. What is
written should seem to be
a happy accident.

—SOMERSET MAUGHAM

Style is to forget all styles.

—JULES RENARD
(contributed by Donna Talarico,
Hippocampus)

Style is knowing who you are,
what you want to say, and not
giving a damn.

—GORE VIDAL

IT IS
NEVER
JUST A
DOG

I am part dog. I have an acute sense of smell. I have to turn around in my basket many times before I go to sleep. I enjoy running and swimming outdoors. I fail to understand what people mean by "bad" weather. A day spent mostly inside makes me grouchy and ill-tempered. Consequently, if I put a dog in a story, it is never just a dog.

MARK HADDON,

author of *The Curious Incident of the Dog in the Night*

WRITING IS...

... **HOW** I understand everything that happens. Writing is the only way I know to move on.

—DELIA EPHRON

... **A** struggle against silence.

—CARLOS FUENTES

... **EASY.** All you have to do is cross out the wrong words.

—MARK TWAIN

. . . **WORK.** Other people can help you a bit, but essentially you're on your own. Nobody is making you do this: you chose it, so don't whine.

—MARGARET ATWOOD

. . . **THINKING** on paper.

—WILLIAM ZINSSER

WRITING WOULD BE EASY IF IT WEREN'T FOR THE DARN WORDS BEING SO UNCOOPERATIVE.

DINTY W. MOORE

I LIKE TO WRITE WHEN I FEEL
SPITEFUL. IT IS LIKE HAVING
A GOOD SNEEZE.

D. H. LAWRENCE
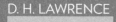

If there's a book that you want to read, but it hasn't been written yet, then you must write it.

—TONI MORRISON

It's the writer's job to stage confrontations, so the characters will say surprising and revealing things, and educate and entertain us all.

—KURT VONNEGUT

Any writer worth his salt writes to please himself . . . it's a self-exploratory operation that is endless. An exorcism of not necessarily his demon, but of his divine discontent.

—HARPER LEE

When writing a novel a writer
should create living people;
people not characters. A
character is a caricature.

—ERNEST HEMINGWAY
(contributed by Sarah Hill, Bookstr)

You can't use up creativity.
The more you use, the more
you have.

—MAYA ANGELOU

The whole magic of a plot
requires that somebody
be impeded from getting
something over with.

—RENATA ADLER

THIS MAY TAKE A WHILE

So this writer walks into a bar. No, make that a writer walks into a dark, smoky bar. No, let's try a writer, looking furtively around the bar, walks into it. That doesn't work, how about a lanky, tanned writer with a prominent chin walks into . . . nope. The bar beckoned to the writer and finally he . . . not that either. OK, the writer, a blank look on his gaunt face, stumbles into. . . . Let me get back to you, this may take a while.

DAVID WAGNER

MAN, SOMETIMES IT TAKES YOU A LONG TIME TO SOUND LIKE YOURSELF.

MILES DAVIS

THE ONLY WAY TO
WRITE IS WELL AND
HOW YOU DO IT IS YOUR
OWN DAMN BUSINESS.

A. J. LIEBLING

I went for years not finishing anything.
Because, of course, when you finish something
you can be judged.

ERICA JONG

ON ADVICE

My six words of advice to writers are:
"Read, read, read,
write, write, write."

ERNEST J. GAINES

There are no writing police.
This is your story, no one
else's. Tell it like you want to.

—RACHEL AARON

Best advice on writing I've
ever received: Finish.

—PETER MAYLE

Writing is a performance, like
singing an aria or dancing a jig.

—STEPHEN GREENBLATT

Your creative should be
expressed through your
writing, not your font.

—NOAH LUKEMAN

There are three rules for
writing a novel. Unfortunately,
no one knows what they are.

—SOMERSET MAUGHAM

I think it's good for a writer
to think he's dying; he works
harder.

—TENNESSEE WILLIAMS

The best advice on writing I've
ever received was, "Rewrite it!"
A lot of editors said that. They
were all right. Writing is really
rewriting—making the story
better, clearer, truer.

—ROBERT LIPSYTE

The correct detail is rarely, exactly, what happened; the most truthful detail is what could have happened, or what should have.

—JOHN IRVING

The good thing about writing fiction is that you can get back at people. I've gotten back at lawyers, prosecutors, judges, law professors, and politicians, I just line 'em up and shoot 'em.

—JOHN GRISHAM

The greatest sin for a writer is to be boring.

—CARL HIAASEN

Make em laugh; make 'em cry; make 'em wait.

—CHARLES READE

When asked, "How do you write?" I invariably answer, "One word at a time," and the answer is invariably dismissed. But that is all it is. It sounds too simple to be true, but consider the Great Wall of China, if you will: one stone at a time, man. That's all. One stone at a time. But I've read you can see that motherfucker from space without a telescope.

STEPHEN KING

Always avoid alliteration.

—UNKNOWN

A synonym is a word you use
when you can't spell the word
you first thought of.

—BURT BACHARACH

The finest language is mostly
made up of simple unimposing
words.

—GEORGE ELIOT

First, have something to say.
Second, say it. Third, stop
when you have said it. Fourth,
give it a good title.

—JOHN SHAW BILLINGS

Always write as if you are
talking to someone. It works.

—MAEVE BINCHY

Almost all good writing begins
with terrible first efforts. You
need to start somewhere.

—ANNE LAMOTT

Write whatever the hell
you want.

—EMMA STRAUB

LISTEN CAREFULLY TO FIRST CRITICISMS MADE OF YOUR WORK. NOTE JUST WHAT IT IS ABOUT YOUR WORK THAT THE CRITICS DON'T LIKE—THEN CULTIVATE IT. THAT'S THE PART OF YOUR WORK THAT'S INDIVIDUAL AND WORTH KEEPING.

JEAN COCTEAU

WRITING HAS LAWS
OF PERSPECTIVE,
OF LIGHT AND SHADE JUST
AS PAINTING DOES, OR
MUSIC. IF YOU ARE BORN
KNOWING THEM, FINE. IF
NOT, LEARN THEM. THEN
REARRANGE THE RULES
TO SUIT YOURSELF.

TRUMAN CAPOTE

Writing and cafés are strongly
linked in my brain.

—J. K. ROWLING

Only those things are
beautiful which are inspired
by madness and written by
reason.

—ANDRÉ GIDE
(contributed by Sarah Hill, *Bookstr*)

Read obsessively.
Write furiously.
Edit carefully.

—UNKNOWN

I have found it helps to pick
out one real person I know and
write to that one person.

—JOHN STEINBECK

The best writing advice I've
ever heard: Don't write like
you went to college.

—ALICE KAHN

You can't let what really
happened tyrannize the
story. The story has its own
demands. It becomes its own
kind of critter and organism,
and you have to listen to that
and its characters.

—JULIA ALVAREZ

Read at the level at which
you want to write. If what you
really love to read is y, it might
be hard for you to write x.

—JENNIFER EGAN

GIVE THE READER AT LEAST ONE CHARACTER HE OR SHE CAN ROOT FOR.

KURT VONNEGUT

It's better to write about things you feel than about things you know about.

—L. P. HARTLEY

An opening line should invite the reader to begin the story. It should say: Listen. Come in here. You want to know about this.

—STEPHEN KING

Breathe in experience, breathe out poetry.

—MURIEL RUKEYSER

Literature is the art of using words. This is not a platitude, but a truth of the first importance. . . .

—ARNOLD BENNETT

WRITE...

... **WHAT** disturbs you, what you fear, what you have not been willing to speak about. Be willing to be split open.

—NATALIE GOLDBERG

... **SOMETHING**, even if it's just a suicide note.

—GORE VIDAL

. . . **SOMETHING** to suit yourself and many people will like it; write something to suit everybody and scarcely anyone will care for it.

—JESSE STUART

. . . **THE** book you would most like to read, but nobody's bothered to write for you.

—PHILIP LARKIN

. . . **ABOUT** something or someone that means so much to you, that you don't care what others think.

—NICK MILLER

Make it dark, make it grim, make it tough, but then, for the love of god, tell a joke.

—JOSS WHEDON

Easy reading is damn hard writing.

—NATHANIEL HAWTHORNE

A little inaccuracy sometimes saves tons of explanation.

—SAKI

There's a hell of a distance between wisecracking and wit. Wit has truth to it; wisecracking is simply calisthenics with words.

—DOROTHY PARKER.

The first draft is just you
telling yourself the story.

—TERRY PRATCHETT

Convince yourself that you are
working in clay not marble, on
paper not eternal bronze: let
that first sentence be as stupid
as it wishes. No one will rush
out and print it as it stands.
Just put it down; then another.

—JACQUES BARZUN

Metaphors have a way of
holding the most truth in the
least space.

—ORSON SCOTT CARD

A metaphor is like a simile.

—AUTHOR UNKNOWN

TRY AGAIN. FAIL AGAIN.
FAIL BETTER.

SAMUEL BECKETT

WHEN IN DOUBT, HAVE A MAN COME THROUGH THE DOOR WITH A GUN IN HIS HAND.

RAYMOND CHANDLER

I get a lot of letters from people. They say: "I want to be a writer. What should I do?" I tell them to stop writing to me and get on with it.

—RUTH RENDELL

Your life is your story.
Write well.
Edit often.

—SUSAN STATHAM

Words are sacred. They deserve respect. If you get the right ones, in the right order, you can nudge the world a little.

—TOM STOPPARD

No tears in the writer,
no tears in the reader.
No surprise for the writer,
no surprise for the reader.

—ROBERT FROST

Creativity requires the courage to let go of certainties.

—ERICH FROMM

The secret of good writing is to say an old thing in a new way or to say a new thing in an old way.

—RICHARD HARDING DAVIS

Writing a book is an adventure. To begin with, it is a toy and an amusement. Then it becomes a mistress, then it becomes a master, then it becomes a tyrant. The last phase is that just as you are about to be reconciled to your servitude, you kill the monster and fling him to the public.

—WINSTON S. CHURCHILL
(contributed by Sarah Hill, *Bookstr*)

My writing advice is read, read, read: you don't have to like what you read but it demystifies writing.

—CHIMAMANDA NGOZI ADICHIE

DON'T...

... **TELL** me the moon is shining; show me the glint of light on broken glass.

—ANTON CHEKHOV

... **PUT** anything in a story that does not reveal character or advance the action.

—KURT VONNEGUT

... **RUSH** or force the ending of a story or book. All you have to know is the next scene.

—CHUCK PALAHNIUK

. . . **BE** afraid to write badly, everyone does.

—FRANK CONROY

(contributed by Dinty Moore, Brevity)

. . . **QUIT**—return home to your writing.

—ELIZABETH GILBERT

. . . **GET** it right, get it written.

—JAMES THURBER

. . . **BE** a "writer." Be writing.

—WILLIAM FAULKNER

Let grammar, punctuation and spelling into your life! Even the most energetic and wonderful mess has to be turned into sentences.

—TERRY PRATCHETT

Inspiration does not come like a bolt, nor is it kinetic energy striving, but it comes to us slowly and quietly and all the time.

—BRENDA UELAND

Get it down. Bumble it through. Tell the story. When you have fifty or a hundred pages typed, you've got something to work with.

—MARY HIGGINS CLARK

You've got to be a good date for the reader.

—KURT VONNEGUT

Hard writing makes easy reading.

—WALLACE STEGNER

Never use a metaphor, simile, or other figure of speech which you are used to seeing in print. **Never** use a long word where a short one will do. If it is possible to cut out a word, always cut it out. **Never** use the passive where you can use the active. **Never** use a foreign phrase, scientific word, or jargon if you can think of an everyday English equivalent. Break any of these rules sooner than say anything outright babarous.

GEORGE ORWELL

Fill your paper with the breathings of your heart.

—WILLIAM WORDSWORTH

Always be on the lookout for the presence of wonder.

—E.B. WHITE

Always carry a notebook. And I mean always. The short-term memory only retains information for three minutes; unless it is committed to paper you can lose an idea for ever.

—WILL SELF

The best prose is that which is most full of poetry.

—VIRGINIA WOOLF

The two most engaging powers of an author are to make new things familiar, familiar things new.

—WILLIAM MAKEPEACE THACKERAY

If you can't annoy somebody, there is little point in writing.

—KINGSLEY AMIS

The art of writing is the art of applying the seat of the pants to the seat of the chair.

—MARY HEATON VORSE

The most valuable of all talents is that of never using two words when one will do.

—THOMAS JEFFERSON

There's a great power in words, if you don't hitch too many of them together.

—JOSH BILLINGS

Tell the whole truth. Don't be lazy, don't be afraid. Close the critic out when you are drafting something new.

—JANE KENYON

Writing is the indelible fingerprint of my soul on paper.

—MICHELLE L. BUCKLEY

Exercise the writing muscle every day,

even if it is only a letter, notes, a title list,

a character sketch, a journal entry.

Writers are like dancers, like athletes.

Without that exercise, the muscles seize up.

JANE YOLEN

Cut out all these exclamation
points. An exclamation point is
like laughing at your own joke.
—F. SCOTT FITZGERALD

Here is a lesson in creative
writing. First rule: Do not
use semicolons. They are
transvestite hermaphrodites
representing absolutely
nothing. All they show is
you've been to college.
—KURT VONNEGUT
(contributed by Sarah Hill, *Bookstr*)

There's not much to be said
about the period except that
most writers don't reach it
soon enough.
—WILLIAM ZINSSER

The idea is to write it so that people hear it and it slides through the brain and goes straight to the heart.

—MAYA ANGELOU

Work on a good piece of writing proceeds on three levels; a musical one, where it is composed; an architectural one, where it is constructed; and finally, a textile one, where it is woven.

—WALTER BENJAMIN

There is only one plot—things are not what they seem.

—JIM THOMPSON

If I ask you to think about something, you can decide not to. But if I make you feel something? Now I have your attention.

—LISA CRON

(contributed by Dinty Moore, *Brevity*)

Be regular and orderly in your life, so that you can be violent and original in your work.

—GUSTAVE FLAUBERT

(contributed by Lee Gutkind, *Creative Nonfiction*)

What is written without effort is in general read without pleasure.

—SAMUEL JOHNSON

Never use the word, "very." It is the weakest word in the English language; doesn't mean anything. If you feel the urge of "very" coming on, just write the word, "damn," in the place of "very." The editor will strike out the word, "damn," and you will have a good sentence.

WILLIAM ALLEN WHITE

People on the outside think there's something magical about writing, that you go up in the attic at midnight and cast the bones and come down in the morning with a story, but it isn't like that. You sit at the typewriter and you work, and that's all there is to it.

HARLAN ELLISON

Normality is a paved road. It's comfortable to walk, but no flowers grow.

—VINCENT VAN GOGH

Words have to be crafted, not sprayed. They need to be fitted together with infinite care.

—NORMAN COUSINS

Verbs are the action words of the language and the most important. Turn to any passage on any page of a successful novel and notice the high percentage of verbs.

—WILLIAM SLOANE

Our admiration of fine writing will always be in proportion to its real difficulty and its apparent ease.

—CHARLES CALEB COLTON

You fail only if you stop writing.

—RAY BRADBURY

An author in his book must
be like God in the universe,
present everywhere and
visible nowhere.

—GUSTAVE FLAUBERT

You can always edit a
bad page. You can't edit
a blank page.

—JODI PICOULT

If you write one story, it may
be bad; if you write a hundred,
you have the odds in your favor.

—EDGAR RICE BURROUGHS

The simpler you say it, the
more eloquent it is.

—AUGUST WILSON

Writing manuals often advise us to "prefer a simpler word to one more complex;" before buying into such counsel, check it against the classics. No writer (and that means also no reader) serious about good work should be so constrained.

—WILLIAM LEAST HEAT-MOON

If proper usage gets in the way, it may have to go. I can't allow what we learned in English composition to disrupt the sound and rhythm of the narrative.

—ELMORE LEONARD
(contributed by Donna Talarico,
Hippocampus)

Tell the readers a story! Because without a story, you are merely using words to prove you can string them together in logical sentences.

—ANNE MCCAFFREY

Write. Don't think. Relax.

—RAY BRADBURY
(contributed by Donna Talarico,
Hippocampus)

Stories move in circles. They don't go in straight lines. So it helps if you listen in circles.

—NAOMI NEWMAN

INSPIRATION IS A GUEST
THAT DOES NOT WILLINGLY
VISIT THE LAZY.

PYOTR TCHAIKOVSKY

WRITING A NOVEL IS LIKE DRIVING A CAR AT NIGHT. YOU CAN ONLY SEE AS FAR AS YOUR HEADLIGHTS, BUT YOU CAN MAKE THE WHOLE TRIP THAT WAY.

E.L. DOCTOROW

REMEMBER: PLOT IS NO MORE THAN FOOTPRINTS LEFT IN THE SNOW AFTER YOUR CHARACTERS HAVE RUN BY ON THEIR WAY TO INCREDIBLE DESTINATIONS.

RAY BRADBURY

Regard yourself as a small corporation of one.

Take yourself off on team-building exercises (long walks).

Hold a Christmas party every year at which you stand in the corner of your writing room, shouting very loudly to yourself while drinking a bottle of wine.

WILL SELF

ON EDITING, REVISION,
AND PUBLICATION

The first draft of anything is shit.

ERNEST HEMINGWAY

Interviewer: How many drafts of a story do you do?

S. J. Perelman: Thirty-seven. I once tried doing thirty-three, but something was lacking, a certain—how shall I say?—*je ne sais quoi*. On another occasion, I tried forty-two versions, but the final effect was too lapidary. . . .

Prune what is turgid, elevate
what is commonplace, arrange
what is disorderly, introduce
rhythm where the language is
harsh, modify where it is too
absolute.

—MARCUS FABIUS
QUINTILIANUS

It is perfectly okay to write
garbage—as long as you edit
brilliantly.

—C. J. CHERRYH

Be grateful for every word you
can cut.

—WILLIAM ZINSSER

No author dislikes to be
edited as much as he dislikes
not to be published.

—RUSSELL LYNES

For your born writer, nothing
is so healing as the realization
that he has come upon the
right word.

—CATHERINE
DRINKER BOWEN

When we finally erect a statue
to the under-appreciated
copyeditor, say in Central
Park, I'll be among the first to
write a check.

—WILLIAM LEAST HEAT-MOON

Vigorous writing is concise. A sentence should contain no unnecessary words, a paragraph no unnecessary sentences, for the same reason that a drawing should have no unnecessary lines and a machine no unnecessary parts.

WILLIAM STRUNK JR.

A good book isn't written, it's rewritten.

—PHYLLIS A. WHITNEY

The best writing is rewriting.

—E.B. WHITE

Rewriting ripens what you've written.

—DUANE ALAN HAHN

The wastebasket is the writer's
best friend.

       —ISAAC BASHEVIS SINGER

A workshop is a way of renting
an audience, and making
sure you're communicating
what you think you're
communicating. It's so easy as
a young writer to think you've
been very clear when in fact
you haven't.

       —OCTAVIA E. BUTLER

Editing might be a bloody
trade. But knives aren't the
exclusive property of butchers.
Surgeons use them too.

       —BLAKE MORRISON

Johann Wolfgang Goethe once wrote a very long letter to one of his friends. In the end he added a postscript explaining, "I am very sorry for sending you such a long letter but I did not find enough time to write a shorter one."

ONE OF THE SIGNS
OF NAPOLEON'S
GREATNESS IS THE FACT
THAT HE ONCE HAD A
PUBLISHER SHOT.

SIEGFRIED UNSELF

Prose is like hair; it shines
with combing.

—GUSTAVE FLAUBERT

As to the adjective, when in
doubt, strike it out.

—MARK TWAIN

The key thing is to get the
stuff down. Once you've got
it, you can revise it, cut it,
expand it or alter it out of all
recognition.

—GILLIAN CROSS

In the writing process, the
more a thing cooks, the better.

—DORIS LESSING

No matter how wonderful a sentence is, if it doesn't add new, useful information it should be removed.

—KURT VONNEGUT

I try to leave out the parts that people skip.

—ELMORE LEONARD

Half my life is an act of revision.

—JOHN IRVING

One method of revision that I find both loathsome and indispensable is reading my work aloud when I'm finished. There are things I can hear— the repetition of words, a particularly flat sentence—that I don't otherwise catch.

—ANN PATCHETT

Sleep on your writing; take a walk over it; scrutinize it of a morning; review it of an afternoon; digest it after a meal; let it sleep in your drawer a twelvemonth; never venture a whisper about it to your friend, if he be an author especially.

A. BRONSON ALCOTT

I was working on the proof of one of my poems all the morning, and took out a comma. In the afternoon I put it back again.

OSCAR WILDE

To write is human,
to edit is divine.

—STEPHEN KING

Revising a story down to the
bare essentials is always a little
like murdering children, but it
must be done.

—STEPHEN KING

I can't write five words but that
I change seven.

—DOROTHY PARKER

You become a good writer
just as you become a good
joiner: by planning down
your sentences.

—ANATOLE FRANCE

My own experience is that
once a story has been written,
one has to cross out the
beginning and the end. It is
there that we authors do most
of our lying.

—ANTON CHEKHOV

Writing a book is like telling
a joke and having to wait two
years to know whether or not
it was funny.

—ALAIN DE BOTTON

A screenwriter returns home after a long evening's work of waiting tables, only to find his house a pile of smoldering rubble. Policemen and firemen poke grimly through the remains. The writer leaps out of his car and runs over to a detective.

"Oh God! My house! What happened? Where are my wife and children?"

The cop says, "I'm sorry sir. I'm afraid your agent came to your house, slaughtered your family, burned your home to the ground, and then danced on the rubble in hobnailed boots."

The writer looks at the detective, eyes wide, excited, and says, "Really? My agent came to my house?"

MICHAEL A. KAHN

IF A WORD IN THE
DICTIONARY WERE
MISSPELLED, HOW
WOULD WE KNOW?

STEVE WRIGHT

No passion in the world is equal to the passion to alter someone else's draft.

—H. G. WELLS

What an author likes to write most is his signature on the back of a cheque.

—BRENDAN BEHAN

The profession of book-writing makes horse racing seem like a solid, stable business.

—JOHN STEINBECK

Do not expect your publisher to advertise your book. Or furnish intelligible royalty statements. Or send the check on time. Or fix the typos in the first edition. Or spell your name right on the jacket.

—HOWARD OGDEN

I was supposed to write a romantic comedy, but my characters broke up.

—ANN BRASHARES

I keep telling young writers I
meet that if they want the sure
road to success, for heaven's
sake, write something that will
make people laugh.

—BENNETT CERF

An editor is a person who
knows more about writing
than writers do but who has
escaped the terrible desire
to write.

E.B. WHITE

Rejection slips, or form letters,
however tactfully phrased, are
lacerations of the soul, if not
quite inventions of the devil—
but there is no way around them.

—ISAAC ASIMOV

Always remember that if
editors were so damned smart,
they would know how to dress.

—DAVE BARRY

GETTING THE FIRST DRAFT FINISHED IS LIKE PUSHING A VERY DIRTY PEANUT ACROSS THE FLOOR WITH YOUR NOSE.

JOYCE CAROL OATES

(contributed by Lee Gutkind, *Creative Nonfiction*)

WHEN VICTOR HUGO
WANTED TO KNOW
WHAT HIS PUBLISHERS THOUGHT
OF HIS MANUSCRIPT FOR
LES MISERABLES, HE SENT
THEM A NOTE READING SIMPLY:
"?"
THEY REPLIED:
"!"

Listen and nod—then put it
back in later.

—WHITNEY BALLIETT,
on editorial advice

Publication is not necessarily
a sign of success.

—WILLIAM SLOANE

The first chapter sells the
book; the last chapter sells the
next book.

—MICKEY SPILLANE

Literature is strewn with the
wreckage of those who have
minded beyond reason the
opinion of others.

—VIRGINIA WOOLF

When someone is mean to me, I just make them a victim in my next book.

—MARY HIGGINS CLARK

The relationship between critic and writer is similar to the one between the pigeon and the statue.

—ASHWIN SANGHI

I do not like to write—I like to have written.

—GLORIA STEINEM

It's easy, after all, not to be a writer. Most people aren't writers, and very little harm comes to them.

—JULIAN BARNES

You know you've read a good book
when you turn the last page and feel
a little as if you have lost a friend.

PAUL SWEENEY

They're fancy talkers about themselves, writers. If I had to give young writers advice, I would say don't listen to writers talk about writing or themselves.

LILLIAN HELLMAN

BEWARE OF ADVICE— EVEN THIS.

CARL SANDBURG

Designer: Hana Anouk Nakamura

Custom Typography by Nick Misani

ISBN: 978-1-4197-3264-5

Foreword © 2018 William Least Heat-Moon

© 2018 Abrams Noterie

Printed and bound in China

10 9 8 7 6 5 4 3

ABRAMS The Art of Books
195 Broadway, New York, NY 10007
abramsbooks.com